Exploring New Heights
CrossPointe #2

Sue Boldt

DEDICATION

To my dear Sistah and Friend, Linda Stanley....

Beautiful lady, your love and passion for knowing and serving Jesus Christ has impacted my life for more years than I care to remember!

Your personal gift of discipling others, no matter the cost to your own comfort, "floors" me every time I think about it. In heaven, there will be countless brothers and sisters who will owe their Journey in Jesus to you!

It is your example that has inspired the CrossPointe Series.

Love in Jesus...
Forever,

Sue Bee

CONTENTS

ACKNOWLEDGMENTS

My aim in the CrossPointe/CrossFire studies is not to write commentary or use commentary from others, unless otherwise noted. My prayer is that the Holy Spirit will illuminate God's word to the participant in who would use this guide in their Journey in Jesus.
Yet…

I'd like to acknowledge my primary study sources unless otherwise noted:

The New Spirit Filled Life Bible
Jack W. Hayford, Litt,.D., Executive Editor, *New Spirit Filled Life Bible*, Nashville, TN: Thomas Nelson, 2002), Word Wealth pg. 1461.

The Key Word Study Bible
Spiros Zodhiates, Th.D., Executive Editor, *The Key Word Study Bible*, New International Version (Chattanooga, TN: AMG Publishers, 1996)

Blue Letter Bible
http://www.blueletterbible.org/

 # Introduction

Exploring New Heights……..

Wow! That sounds amazing…but…maybe reaching for higher plateaus might mean reaching outside of my comfort zone. Hmmmph! What to do?

And yet, the shouts of laughter, the giggling of glee, the whoops of joy from those who can see from the mountaintops is enough to make us want to turn off Facebook and see what is causing all the ruckus!!

God is always calling us to come higher; closer to Him. It is not that He isn't everywhere; but He is always calling us to look up to Him, to know that He has a perspective on our lives that we can't possibly fathom. From His vantage point, He can see things that we can't. He is inviting us to join Him.

Moses met God on a mountain; David worshiped God on a mountain; Elijah talked with God on a mountain; Elisha saw the armies of God on a mountain; and Jesus went to the mountains to be with the Father. There is something to be said about having a view that rises above the norm. And that is what God has in store for us. And yes, we will be stretched out of our comfort zone.

We are on a lifelong Journey with the God of the Universe. And, what an astounding Journey it is. Individually custom-designed for us by the Lord, Who gave His life for us; He is now beckoning us to join Him on higher ground.

In CrossPointe #1 (CrossFire #1 for guys!) we studied the basics of the Christian Faith: God's Love, His Word, The Power of the Cross, Assurance, Powerful New Life, Refreshing Streams, Changing Directions, and Light in the Darkness.

In CrossPointe #2 we will continue the adventure. We will meet the relatives, change flat tires, learn new car tunes, get in over our heads, open treasure chests, and, of course, stand on mountaintops.

Will it sometimes be a bumpy road? You betcha!

Will it have some twists and turns? What journey doesn't!

Will it be worth it? This is the trip of a lifetime that most people only dream about, but you have a personalized invitation to come.

So, find one or two partners to join you on this portion of your Journey. Try to meet once a week; not letting two weeks go by without getting together. But, if this doesn't happen, no guilt is allowed! Just jump back on the "tour bus" as soon as you are able.

Come prepared, having completed the study. Begin with prayer and answering the opening questions at the beginning of the chapter you just studied. Then, discuss the highlights of the lesson you just completed. Use the margins or "Notes" section at the back of each chapter to record extra thoughts that touch your heart.

If you like, do the study together instead of preparing ahead of time. Whatever you decide, ask questions, talk, laugh, cry, listen, and most of all; hear from Jesus' heart to your own heart.

Last of all, be sure to use a version of the Bible that *you* understand! The New King James Version (NKJV) is used throughout the CrossPointe series, unless otherwise noted. Sometimes, it is handy to use that version to get the full gist of the questions, but it certainly is not required. (Hey! Download a NKJV Bible app on your phone to use along with your favorite Bible version.)

Are you ready to roll? Do you have your hiking boots, lipstick, and compact? (Gotta carry the essentials, you know!) Well, let's get moving and explore those exhilarating mountaintops!

> *"How beautiful upon the mountains*
> *Are the feet of him who brings good news,*
> *Who proclaims peace,*
> *Who brings glad tidings of good things,*
> *Who proclaims salvation,*
> *Who says to Zion,*
> ***"Your GOD reigns!"***
> Isaiah 52:7

In the Company
of Travelers

~The Fulfillment of Fellowship~

Together Time

- Open your time together in prayer.

- Share with each other a meaningful time of fellowship with other believers that you have recently experienced.

- Share about a recent time of being in the Lord's presence by yourself that encouraged your heart.

- Discuss the highlights of the study you just completed.

Lesson:

Perhaps you are having the most amazing life experience...but no one is there to share it with you.

It's kind of like going to Disneyland...all alone.

Oh my...that doesn't sound so great or like very much fun.

Possibly you have a huge decision to make, and though you are fairly certain that God is telling you what to do, it would be helpful to have some extra encouragement or wisdom to confirm what you are hearing.

Or, maybe you have often traveled upon certain "roads" on the Journey of Life with Jesus, but you have just turned a corner and you have no prior experience with what you now face. It would be great to have someone with expertise who has traveled around this bend with God to tell you what they learned.

> *"For where two or three are gathered together in My name, I am there in the midst of them."*
> Matthew 18:20

God "wired" us to need each other. No, He didn't wire us to put any person before Him in importance, but the very core of the Godhead: Father, Son, and Spirit, is relational. He never intended for Christians to be "Lone Rangers." We were meant to be on this adventure with others; exploring and realizing the depths of God's love as a family...even with the quirky relatives!!

In Old Testament times God used the nation of Israel to demonstrate His love for all of mankind. This nation was birthed by faith in God's promises to Abraham regarding his descendents. It was out of Abraham's family that the twelve tribes of Israel came to be. And, to tell the truth, they weren't all that great of a family! That gives us all hope!

- Read Exodus 19:3-7. List some of the statements that God tells Moses to say to Israel.
    - _____
    - _____
    - _____

■ _____

In the New Testament Peter tells us about the "church;" those who are now God's people through faith in Jesus Christ:

> *"But you are a chosen generation, a royal priesthood, a holy nation. His own special people, that you may proclaim the praises of Him who called you out of darkness into His marvelous light;*
>
> *who once were not a people but are now the people of God, who had not obtained mercy but now have obtained mercy."*
> 1 Peter 2:9-10

• From the Exodus 19:3-7 passage and the verses above, list three similarities:

    ■ _____

    ■ _____

    ■ _____

God loves us individually, make no mistake about that! However, He also loves us collectively, or as a family. "Family" is the heart of God. (That is one reason why the Lord so vehemently despises divorce *Malachi 2:16*.) Throughout the Old Testament, God continually called His people to meet with Him, celebrate Him, worship Him, confess and repent of their sins, and perform the atoning sacrifices…together.

• Read Psalm 133. Keeping verse 1 the same, re-write verses 2 and 3 with contemporary word pictures that are meaningful to you!

_____

_____

_____

_____

_____

_____

_____

• Turn back a few pages to Psalm 122:1-2. What does King David say makes him glad or happy to do?

_____

In the Old Testament God met with His people, first in a huge tent or tabernacle when they were traveling to the Promised Land; then in a beautiful temple that King Solomon originally built. Jewish life, culture, and their relationship with God centered around the temple. God's presence resided in the temple, however, only the Hebrew high priests and relatively few others, experienced Him.

Now, because of the life, death, and resurrection of Jesus, we know God's presence by His Holy Spirit dwelling in us!

> *"But he who is joined to the Lord is one spirit with Him.*
> *Flee sexual immorality. Every sin that a man does is outside the body, but he who commits sexual immorality sins against his own body.*
> *Or do you not know that your body is the temple of the Holy Spirit who is in you, whom you have from God, and you are not your own?*
> *For you were bought at a price; therefore glorify God in your body and in your spirit, which are God's."*
> 1 Corinthians 6:17-20

We are getting to the heart of the matter. We are God's temple; His dwelling place. We no longer go to a temple, we **are** His temple. Together, with all Christians around the world we are called His "church." What does the original Greek word for "church" mean?

Ekklesia Greek – Meaning: Called out, assembly, a gathering, a gathered body, community, church; a common term for a congregation of those called out or assembled.

When Jesus told the multitudes that he would build His own *Ekklesia*, the Jews knew exactly what He meant. Jesus was claiming His Lordship and deity. His church would be a continuation of the nation of Israel; now incorporating all people who would proclaim Him "Lord."

Today, the church is not a building; it is the people who comprise God's family. We don't *go* to church; we *are* the church.

- Read Matthew 16:15-19. What does Simon (Peter) say in verse 16? _____

  _____

- From the same passage what does Jesus say about His church in verses 18 and 19?

  _____

  _____

  _____

In this passage, Jesus gives Simon the name *Peter* or *Petros*. The Greek meaning of this word is *little rock or stone*. However, the Greek word for *rock*, *Petra*, that Jesus uses to describe the foundation of His church, means *large stone or boulder*. Jesus is not building His church upon the man, Peter, but on the truth that He (Jesus) is the Christ (Messiah), the Son of God. Jesus, and the truth of Who He is the Rock that we stand upon today, and the gates of hell cannot prevail against us, His church!

- Turn again to 1 Peter 2. Now, read verses 1-7. What does it mean to you to be called a living stone, just as Peter was named?

  _____

_____

_____

- From the same passage, what are believers again called, that we have read about earlier in this chapter?

  _____

- Now from verses 6 and 7, Who is the Chief Cornerstone?

  _____

Jesus calling Peter *little stone* must have had a huge impact on this disciple. Peter realized that he was a *little stone* of a *Larger Rock*; a larger "picture" than just his own individual life. Now, in his letter to the early church, Peter shares with us that we are **all** *living stones* being built up to make a spiritual house where we are **all** called to be priests. What importance and value this gives to our lives in regard to the local church body and the larger global church! We are all important and we are all needed! Have you ever seen a stone or brick house with a missing piece? That missing piece of rock or brick weakens the entire structure. Yes, you and I are needed.

- We see the early church in action in Acts 2:42-47. Read the passage and choose four phrases that touch your heart about the *ekklesia* in Jerusalem:
  - _____
  - _____
  - _____
  - _____

Paul brings another huge dimension to the meaning of *church*:

> *"For as the body is one and has many*
> *members, but all the members of that one body,*
> *being many, are one body, so also is Christ.*
> *For by one Spirit we were all baptized into*

*one body – whether Jews or Greeks, whether
slaves or free – and have all been made to
drink into one Spirit.*
    *For in fact the body is not one member but
many.*
1 Corinthians 12:12-4

*"Now you are the body of Christ, and
members individually."*
1 Corinthians 12:27

We are not just another club or social network; we are the **Body of Christ** on this planet! We are God's family; God's "called out" ones.

This means that we are to love every member of His body...and, oh my...this can be an *issue*. Loving each other isn't always easy. Yet, this is one major way that the Lord Jesus transforms us into His image.

*"As iron sharpens iron, so a man sharpens the
countenance of his friend."*
Proverbs 27:17

- What do you think this verse means?

_____

_____

_____

How we care, react, treat, forgive, encourage, and love other members of Christ's body is crucial to our growth as Christians. We can talk about caring for each other, but the "rubber meets the road" when we actually have to love someone difficult who is a Christian. Because God's Holy Spirit is dwelling inside of us, when we allow Him to, His love can take over where our fleshly love fails. This is an act of laying our selfishness aside.

- Turn to the middle portion of the verses from the preceding page, 1 Corinthians 12:15-26. Summarize what you think Paul is saying here:

_____

_____

_____

_____

_____

_____

_____

- Just for fun, what "body part" are you in Jesus' church? Explain!

_____

_____

_____

_____

We read about the early church in Acts 2:42:

> *"And they continued steadfastly in the apostles' doctrine and fellowship, in the breaking of bread, and in prayers."*

The word *fellowship* is a key ingredient in life as a church. What does this word mean in the original New Testament language?

Koinonia Greek – Meaning: sharing, unity, close association, partnership, participation, a communion, a community, a fellowship, contributing help, a brotherhood.

We are told by almost every New Testament writer that our *koinonia* should always be with people of "light," walking in the Light, and not of "darkness." This of course doesn't mean that we don't love, reach out to, or associate with non-Christians. However, it does mean that our closest fellowship, comfort, guidance, and strength should come from the Lord's family.

Paul understands Jesus' heart for His body, the church. Paul also understands true *koinonia*. In his letter to the church at Ephesus, Paul gives the blueprint and the desired outcome for the local body of believers in that city. It is the same blueprint and outcome for our local church that we belong to today.

- Read Ephesians 4:1-16. Answer the questions for the verses given below.

- Verses 2-3. How are we to act towards each other?

  _____

  _____

- Verses 11-15. What is the goal of the ministry gifts (apostles, prophets, pastors) for the church?

  _____

  _____

  _____

  _____

  _____

- Verse 16. How does this verse challenge you?

  _____

  _____

  _____

  _____

We are all on this journey with Jesus together. Sometimes it will seem easier to "go it" alone. As with any road trip, there are stops and starts, frequent potty breaks, snack runs, someone gets cranky, another forgets where the tour bus is parked, disagreement about where to eat lunch, and who stole someone else's bus seat or misplaced the keys.

But face it, any memorable road trip, any journey; and especially this most important adventure with Christ, was never meant to be taken alone. We *need* each other. Those of us who have put our faith in Him, cannot fully grow up in Jesus without the care, nurture, sharpening, and love of the other members of His body. He did that on purpose. We need Him to help us be His body that is "knit together in love."

So…grab your bag of Cheetos along with your can of Coke, and jump on board. You don't want to miss this wild and exciting ride with the family. The Adventure is just more fun, exciting, comforting, enjoyable, and rewarding in the company of these travelers!

"A new commandment I give to you, that you love one another; as I have loved you, that you also love one another.

By this all will know that you are My disciples, if you have love for one another."
John 13:34-35

"And let us consider one another in order to stir up love, and good works,

not forsaking the assembling of ourselves together, as is the manner of some, but exhorting one another, and so much the more as you see the Day approaching."
Hebrews 10:24-25

 # Notes

Car Tunes

~The Wonder of Worship~

Together Time:

- Begin your time together in prayer.

- Share with one another how your journey with the Lord is going right now.

- Has learning or remembering about worship been helpful to your times alone with the Lord and in your times with other believers?

- Have you tried a new expression of worship, either alone or with others? If so, how did it touch your heart?

- Share highlights from the lesson below.

Lesson:

A lot of life's problems would be easily solved if we just realized that God is God, and we...well...we're not God.

That is pretty much the sum total of what **worship** means.

It is also a reminder to our adversary that he is not God, either.

Every human on this planet worships. Who or what they worship is the divine gift of "free will" or "free choice." But make no mistake about it...everyone worships someone or something.

True worship of the living God is the best, highest, noblest, beneficial activity we can ever engage in. It is probably one of the most thrilling and downright "fun" things we can do, as well. When our spirits engage the power of the Holy Spirit to bring God praise, we are changed. On this Journey of Life in Jesus, "traveling down the road," these "car tunes" of praise will bring such delight to our emotions, encourage our faith, and bring us into His very presence in such a way that we will wonder why we don't participate in it more, especially when we are alone with Him.

- Read Mark 12:28-30. What does Jesus state is the first commandment?

  _____

  _____

  _____

  _____

- Answer what it means for you to love and worship God with all of your:

  Heart:

  _____

  _____

  Soul:

  _____

  _____

Mind:

_____

_____

Strength:

_____

_____

Worshiping God is for *us*. God is not insecure or in need of affirmation. He is not "needy" or "high maintenance." When we declare the greatness of the Lord, it opens our souls (our emotions; our hearts), our minds (our intellect and understanding; where we make choices), and even our bodies (our strength) to the presence of God. Worship takes our eyes off of ourselves, who are finite and full of limitations; and onto God, Who is infinite and limitless. True worship raises our sights from the impossible to the possible. And yes, because it is often an act of faith, real worship blesses His heart.

- Read about the first mention of *worship* in the Old Testament in Genesis 22:1-18. Take time to answer this question. What does Abraham's actions speak to your heart about worship?

_____

_____

_____

_____

_____

_____

Worship is more than just singing with the band at church on Sunday mornings. It is even more than our alone times with the Lord, speaking praise to Him. These are amazing and significant aspects of our Journey with Christ. However, first and foremost, worship is a way of life. It is how we live day-by-day, 24-7-365.

"I beseech you therefore, brethren, by the

*mercies of God, that you present your bodies a
living sacrifice, holy, acceptable to God, which
is your reasonable service."*
Romans 12:1

The word *service* in the verse above does mean a physical act, but it also means *worship*. Our surrender of every aspect of our lives is worship. Not keeping God in one compartment of our lives, actions, and emotions; but giving Him complete control over every aspect of our being. However, the "problem" with our being *a living sacrifice* to God is that we keep crawling off the altar! Genuine praise and worship reminds us of who truly is God!

Remember reading about the Vine and the branches in John 15? (CrossPointe #1)

• Read John 15:8. What glorifies God here?

_____

_____

_____

No guilt here – only encouragement! In and of ourselves, we can't make *fruit*. It's only as we rest, abide, trust, and surrender to Jesus that causes us to have lives that bring God glory; bring Him worship.

The 150 Psalms of the Old Testament are by and large, songs of praise. Think of them as a "medicine cabinet" when you need a good dose of encouragement or faith.

• Read Psalm 100. What is the most meaningful verse(s) to you? Write it out.

_____

_____

_____

_____

"But you are holy,
Enthroned in the praises of Israel."
Psalm 22:3

God is always with us, however, in worship, **we** become more **aware** of His presence. Worship is like dialing in perfectly to get the best reception of a radio station. Perhaps a better analogy for worship is like having "all the bars" when using our cell phones! When we worship, distractions flee and we become tuned into God. We actually feel and sense His presence. That is a huge faith builder. We don't worship Him to get sensations, but the overflow of the Holy Spirit is present in the midst of true worship. He is enthroned upon our praises.

Let's look at some ways we can express worship as seen in the Psalms.

- Look up each verse and record how worship is being expressed (there may be more than one expression):

- Psalm 27:6 _____

- Psalm 35:27 _____

- Psalm 35:28 _____

- Psalm 47:1 _____

- Psalm 63:4 _____

- Psalm 95:6 _____

- Psalm 150:4 _____

In John 4:1-30, Jesus encounters a woman "with a past" at a well in

Samaria. After revealing to her that He knows everything about her, she realizes that Jesus is the long-awaited Messiah, or Savior. Because the Samaritans were hated by the Jews, they were excluded from temple life and worship in Jerusalem. The woman questions Jesus about worship in verse 20.

> *"Jesus said to her, "Woman, believe Me, the hour is coming when you will neither on this mountain, nor in Jerusalem, worship the Father.*
>
> *You worship what you do not know; we know what we worship, for salvation is of the Jews.*
>
> *But the hour is coming, and now is, when the true worshipers will worship the Father in spirit and truth; for the Father is seeking such to worship Him.*
>
> *God is Spirit, and those who worship Him must worship in spirit and truth."*
> John 4:21-24

• Explain what you think it means to worship Him in *spirit and truth*.

_____

_____

_____

_____

In John 16:14 we learn that the Holy Spirit glorifies Jesus. The Holy Spirit ignites our spirits to bring an element of wonder and power when we speak, sing, or shout praise to God. To worship God in truth means to worship with sincerity of heart. To put it bluntly, God knows when we are faking it!

• Read Matthew 15:7-8. Jesus is quoting Isaiah 29:13 here. Consider Jesus' words carefully, what is speaking to your *heart*

- from these verses?

_____

_____

_____

_____

_____

Jesus is warning us of the peril of slowly drifting in our hearts from being fully in love with Him, and from being engaged in a vital relationship with Him. Much like in a marriage, when a spouse is merely going through the motions of life together, but the heart has grown cold. Intimacy is waning or has been lost.

Losing intimacy with God is what happened to the religious scribes and Pharisees whom Jesus was talking to. When you find yourself on "auto-pilot" in worshipping God, it is time to take notice of your heart. A good question to ask yourself is: "Have I been careful to have alone time with the Lord, experiencing His presence and His words to me?"

There will be times in our lives when the last thing we *feel* like doing is worshipping the Lord. These times may be due to adversity, tragedy, or struggle. It is in these instances that we *most* need to focus on His greatness. At these dark times we truly need to "switch on" the light and power of the Lord Jesus in our hearts and minds through praise. In the midst of suffering, our declaring His Lordship is an act of our faith and is a true *sacrifice of praise*, as the author of Hebrews writes:

> *"Therefore by Him let us continually offer the sacrifice of praise to God, that is, the fruit of our lips, giving thanks to His name."*
> Hebrews 13:15

- Read Philippians 4:6-7. What is Paul's *cure* for anxiety?

_____

_____

_____

- From the same passage, re-write into your own words, the promise found in verse 7:

_____

_____

_____

_____

- What does that promise mean to you?

_____

_____

_____

_____

Psalm 149 gives us the final benefit of worship that we will look at. Below are a few verses from this short psalm:

> *"Praise the Lord!*
> *Sing to the Lord a new song...*
> *...Let the high praises of God be in their mouth,*
> *And a two-edged sword in their hand,*
> *To execute vengeance on the nations,*
> *And punishments on the peoples.*
> *To bind their kings with chains,*
> *And their nobles with fetters of iron;*
> *To execute on them the written judgment –*
> *This honor have all His saints.*
> *Praise the Lord!"*

Worshipping God is a form of spiritual warfare against our adversary, the devil. Because worship ushers in God's presence, the enemy flees at the sound of praise. When Psalm 149 speaks of *binding kings and nobles* it means the demonic realm that would seek to enslave men's hearts and minds *Ephesians 6:12*.

As stated before, worship builds our faith as we declare the power of our God, and faith always overcomes the enemy.

> *"...above all, taking the shield of faith with which you will be able to quench all the fiery darts of the wicked one."*
> Ephesians 6:16

> *"For whatever is born of God overcomes the world. And this is the victory that has overcome the world – our faith."*
> 1 John 5:4

In 2 Chronicles 20:1-30, we find the story of Judah and Jerusalem under attack by several nearby nations. King Jehoshaphat calls his nation together to seek the Lord. At the end of the beautiful prayer, God speaks through the prophet Jahaziel and tells the people not to be afraid.

- Read 2 Chronicles 20:15-25. Answer the questions below:

- Does God tell them to form a SWAT team? _____

- Does He tell them to get better life insurance? _____

- What does He tell them to do in verse 17?

  _____

  _____

  _____

  _____

  _____

  _____

- What does Jehoshaphat encourage the people to do in verse 20?

  _____

  _____

- What *act of warfare* do they do in verse 21? _____

  _____

- What is the outcome in verses 23-25?

  _____

  _____

  _____

  _____

  _____

Worship is what we give *worth* to: **worth-ship**. When "push comes to shove," where most of our thoughts, time, and energy are expended on is what we worship. Remember reading about our heart, mind, and strength earlier in the chapter? No condemnation or guilt, here. We are on a journey and we grow with every mile that passes. However, when we keep our hearts and minds on the greatness of our God through praise, any *valleys* we may go through can become *mountain top* experiences.

Genuine, Spirit-filled worship can turn a ho-hum work day into a great adventure, a milk-run to the market into soaring on new heights, and folding clothes in the laundry room into being in God's glorious presence. The *car tunes* on our journey can even defeat our enemy!

Pretty amazing stuff! How about taking a moment right now and putting fresh words of love on our lips to our Wonderful King!

"Let my mouth be filled with Your praise
And with Your glory all the day."
Psalm 71:8

 # Notes

When He Calls Your Name

~Hearing His Voice~

Together Time:

- Open in prayer inviting Jesus to speak to your hearts during your time together.

- Share something that Lord has been doing in your life this past month.

- Is there a particular Bible verse that has recently been very meaningful to you?

- Share your notes from the lesson below.

Lesson:

One of the most thrilling aspects of the Christian adventure is hearing God speak directly to you.

One of the most challenging aspects of the Christian adventure is trying to figure out if it was actually God that spoke to you and not the reaction to eating an over-sized Chipotle carnitas-burrito with extra sour cream, guacamole, pinto beans, fajita vegetables, and hot salsa!

Regardless if you have difficulty in believing that the God of the universe wants to have a personal conversation with you (original Pointer Sistah, Eileen Santa Ana, likens it to making a "date" with Him at Starbucks: intimate, warm, and personal), the Bible teaches this truth continually from Genesis to Revelation.

> *"My sheep hear My voice, and I know them,*
> *and they follow Me."*
> John 10:27

It is imperative that we, Jesus' lambs, learn to hear, listen for, and discern His voice. We can't genuinely follow Him if we don't know what His voice sounds like. The enemy, the world, everyone around us, and our own flesh are constantly speaking to us, but it is only His voice that truly matters.

Beginning with Adam in the Book of Genesis, all the way to the Apostle John in the Book of Revelation, the Lord is continually speaking to individuals. And, these are not perfect individuals either! Nothing has changed: it is God's heart to communicate His love, plans, and counsel to anyone who will listen; even to those whom He knows **won't** listen!

- Read Deuteronomy 30:11-14. List what Moses says about hearing God's voice (commands for abundant living):
  - _____
  - _____
  - _____
  - _____

God wants us to hear His voice. He desires to have a two-way conversation with us and we don't have to "reach for the moon" to have this dialogue. For most of us, conversing with God means giving Him our "laundry list" of prayer requests. We may not even stop to hear what He might have to say to us. Yet, He has much to tell us. He longs to speak to us regarding how much He loves us, would comfort and encourage us, give us guidance and direction, and get us back on the "right track" when we have drifted. He has much to say to us *daily* about living as His most precious sons and daughters; the apple of His eye and the prize of His heart.

There are immeasurable benefits in hearing God's voice. The first benefit is the unspeakable joy that it brings knowing that He loves you so much that He delights in talking to *you* (all by yourself, nobody else!). Talk about building and encouraging your sense of worth!

> *"But now, thus says the Lord, who created you, O Jacob, And He who formed you, O Israel: "Fear not, for I have redeemed you; I have called you by your name; you are Mine.""*
> Isaiah 43:1

- Read the verse above a few more times putting your name in place of Jacob's and Israel's name (we did this in CrossPointe #1). How does this touch your heart?

  _____

  _____

  _____

  _____

- Turn to Isaiah 55:1-3. What do these verses say about *how* to hear God?

  _____

  _____

  _____

- From the same passage, what are the promises given about

29

listening to His voice? (Remember, our souls are the place of our emotions, will, and intellect.)

_____

_____

_____

_____

_____

Isaiah is reminding us that we all work so crazy-hard to obtain things that do not satisfy us in the long-run. He encourages us that if we would put all of that wasted effort into drawing near, listening carefully to, and inclining our ears towards God's voice, our hearts will have everything we could ever desire. We will experience true abundance and satisfaction on life's journey!

Though it is obvious what blessings can be derived from hearing God's voice personally, let's look at a few that the Bible gives us. List them below:

• Psalm 107:20

_____

_____

• Psalm 119:98 (Commands = His words):

_____

_____

• Isaiah 30:21

_____

_____

• Isaiah 48:15-17

_____

_____

- John 16:13

  _____

  _____

- Revelation 3:20

  _____

  _____

The last passage we just read out of Revelation is the most exquisite and best of all of the promises: a personal invitation to spend time with Jesus, heart to heart. Time alone with Him is truly like sharing a meal with Him: we come away from His presence having our every longing satisfied; having heard Him speak to us through His written word or to our hearts directly. It is also true that nothing will sharpen our ability to hear His voice better, than our times in sweet fellowship with Him.

- Share what came to your heart and mind after you read Revelation 3:20.

  _____

  _____

  _____

  _____

  _____

Everyday, our Journey of Life in Jesus will be different from the day before. Jesus can and will speak to us in a variety of ways that we may miss if we are not looking or hearing expectantly. Let's look at just a few *ways* He spoke to people in the New Testament. List these ways found in the passages below:

- Matthew 1:20 _____

- Acts 16:6-10 _____

- Acts 21:10-11 _____

- 1 Corinthians 14:3 _____

- 1 Corinthians 14:26 (How God might speak in a meeting of Christians): _____

When we look at the Old and New Testaments of the Bible, we learn that God spoke to individuals through nature, His audible voice, an impression on the heart, through people, through His written word, through circumstances, dreams, visions, angels...even a donkey! Our God is *out-of-the box* when He works and speaks. Don't dismiss even the tiniest or most fantastic ways He might be trying to communicate with you. You don't want to miss a *love-letter* from Him in your everyday life!

But, what does God's voice sound like? How do we discern His voice from our own thoughts, the enemy's voice, and a big, bad burrito?

How the Lord speaks to us individually is a very subjective matter, as unique as each of our individual relationships with Him. However, the Bible does give us several helpful hints.

> *"Do not think that I came to destroy the Law or the Prophets. I did not come to destroy but to fulfill.*
> *For assuredly, I say to you, till heaven and earth pass away, one jot or one tittle will by no means pass from the law till all is fulfilled."*
> Matthew 5:17-18

Pastor Randy Boldt teaches that God probably speaks to us 90% of the time directly from His written word, the Bible. First and foremost, God will not violate His written word. God is unchanging; He does not change His words *James 1:17, Hebrews 13:8.* Jesus tells us that His word is truth *John 17:17*; and that it is eternal *1 Peter 1:25.*

When Jesus walked the earth, He didn't throw out the Old Testament, He fulfilled it *Matthew 5:17.* The Bible is the perfect litmus test for judging whether the Lord has really spoken to you. If a *word from the Lord* comes to you doesn't pass the simple test of aligning with the Scriptures, you can "chalk it up" to someone else's voice. This test also shows the great importance of knowing the Bible for yourself: inside-out and backwards!

The prophet Elijah was in the midst of a "pity party." Having just been a part of a huge miracle revealing God's might, he was discouraged because the evil queen of Israel put out a death warrant for him *1 Kings 18-19.* Elijah hid in a cave where he and the Lord had a conversation.

> *"The He said, "Go out, and stand on the mountain before the Lord." And behold, the Lord passed by, and a great and strong wind tore into the mountains and broke the rocks in pieces before the Lord, but the Lord was not in the wind; and after the wind an earthquake, but the Lord was not in the earthquake; and after the earthquake a fire, but the Lord was not in the fire; and after the fire a still small voice."*
> 1 Kings 19:11-12

- List all the "big" things that God was *not* in:
  - _____
  - _____
  - _____

- How did God's voice finally sound to Elijah?
  _____

This famous passage in 1 Kings gives us a clear directive about hearing God speak to us personally. The original Hebrew words for *still* and *small* are

Demamah Hebrew – Meaning: Silence, stillness, calm, a whisper

Dak Hebrew – Meaning: Thin, small, lean-fleshed, dwarf, a little thing.

The New International Version of the Bible translates this phrase as *a gentle whisper.*

- What does God speaking in a *still small voice* mean to you?

_____

_____

_____

_____

_____

The Lord will not compete for our attention. Our lives are filled with big, noisy sounds and voices that often draw our attention away from Him.

Popular author and speaker, Margaret Feinberg, states the following in her book, *Hungry for God*:

> *"Instead of filling the solar system with Star Wars presentations, carving words in tree bark, or dropping parchment from the sky, God whispers in order to draw us closer."**

Yes, God does use a loud voice sometimes, make no mistake about that! But His gentle, quiet voice seems to be how He most often speaks to us.

- What things in your life are big and noisy and distract you from hearing God's voice sometimes?

  _____

  _____

  _____

  _____

  _____

- What are some changes you could make to better hear the Lord's voice?

  _____

  _____

  _____

  _____

Randy Boldt also notes that often the words the Lord speaks to our hearts are small and compact. He unwraps these words to us like a present. One phrase from God can have volumes of meaning, and the Holy Spirit is most gracious to unwrap or give the explanation to us _John 16:13_.

James gives us two important clues to discerning Jesus' voice from the world's or the devil's voices.

- Read James 3:13-17. List the ways God's voice **_doesn't_** sound like from verse 16:

  _____

  _____

  _____

- Now, from verse 17, list what the Lord's voice **_does_** sound like:

  _____

  _____

  _____

  _____

"And they said to one another, "Did not our heart burn within us while He talked with us on the road, and while He opened the Scriptures to us?"
Luke 24:32

"For the word of God is living and powerful, and sharper than any two-edged sword, piercing even to the division of soul and spirit, and of joints and marrow, and is a discerner of the thoughts and intents of the heart."
Hebrews 4:12

Clearly, when Jesus speaks to us it affects our hearts and minds, whether it is something small, or something life-changing. Even if His words are challenging or correcting us, He is able to encourage us and "warm" our hearts. Any words of condemnation are not from Him *Romans 8:1*.

In the story of Paul's voyage to Rome *Acts 27*, we have a clearly written description of the various ways that Jesus might speak to us today on our Journey of Life. We might be tempted to say, "Oh, that was Paul, and I'll never be like him!" No, you will be like...**you**! A beloved child that the Lord wants to speak to daily. He may use His written word, an impression on your heart, a picture in your mind, a friend, a beautiful sunset, even a TV show (remember the donkey in the Old Testament!) to speak words of direction, correction, love, encouragement, comfort, joy, or regarding a future event.

On this adventure we're taking, it is all important to become accustomed to hearing Jesus' voice. We don't want to miss anything He has to say specifically to us. In this crazy cell-phone-texting-Twittering-Facebooking-Linkedin-world, many are trying to snare our attention. Jesus still speaks to His lambs, and more than ever, His lambs need to hear His voice to follow Him on His path to higher heights.

There is no thrill on earth that surpasses the sound of His voice...

> *"But he who enters by the door is the shepherd of the sheep.*
> *To him the doorkeeper opens, and the sheep hear his voice; and he calls his own sheep by name and leads them out.*
> *And when he brings out his own sheep, he goes before them; and the sheep follow him, for they know his voice.*
> *Yet they will by no means follow a stranger, but will flee from him, for they do not know the voice of strangers."*
> John 10:2-5

> *"I am the good shepherd; and I know My sheep, and am known by My own."*
> John 10:14

* Margaret Feinberg, *Hungry for God*, (Grand Rapids, MI: Zondervan, 2011), page 15. Used with permission.

 # Notes

Discovering
Delight

~The Joy of Surrender~

Together Time:

- Ask the Lord for a "special" time of encouragement together.

- Apart from the Lord, what is your greatest delight in life? Take time to describe how this delight makes you feel inside.

- If you are willing, no pressure, share with each other something that is difficult for you to keep surrendered to the Lord and His will. Encourage one another.

- Share your notes from the lesson below. Jot down important things that are said during your time together.

Lesson:

Hmmmmmmm....discovering delight.

What is your heart's delight? Somehow that English word produces thoughts of...well...delight! How about a definition:

Noun: A high degree of pleasure or enjoyment; joy; rapture, something that gives great pleasure.

Verb: To give great pleasure, satisfaction, or enjoyment to, to please highly.

The Old Testament definitions for two Hebrew words that are translated *delight* are:

Hapes Hebrew – Meaning: to find pleasure in, delight in, be pleased with, to have affection for; to desire, choose.   Denotes a strong positive attraction for something or someone as demonstrated by both God and men.

Anag Hebrew – Meaning: to be soft, to be delicate, to be happy about, to take exquisite delight, to make merry over.

A beautiful promise is found in a string of promises in Psalm 37:

> *"Delight yourself also in the Lord,*
> *And He shall give you the desires of your*
> *heart."*
> Psalm 37:4

- Recalling the definitions regarding *delight*, what do you think it means to *delight in the Lord*?

_____

_____

_____

This short promise speaks volumes regarding our Journey in Jesus. Simply put: when we truly delight in the Lord, making Him the main focus of our affection and pleasure, we will find that **He** *is* the desire of our heart!

- Read Isaiah 58:13-14. Focus on the last few lines of verse 13 and list what it means to *delight* yourself in the Lord:
  1. _____
  2. _____
  3. _____
  4. _____

- Now, number by number from your list above, write what each phrase means to you:
  1. _____
  2. _____
  3. _____
  4. _____

- Re-write in your own words the Lord's promise found in verse 14:

  _____

  _____

  _____

  _____

This chapter is probably the most important chapter in the entire CrossPointe Series. If you have reached this fourth chapter in the second CrossPointe book, it is assumed that you have already made a decision to receive Jesus' work on the cross and accept His forgiveness for your sins. You are a born-again believer in Christ *John 3:3*; you are a Christian.

However, there is more.

More that God wants you to experience of Him...
        Of His goodness and power.
                More of Himself that He desires to reveal...
                        to your heart and mind.
There are greater adventures to experience...

on His amazing Journey of Life.

More of the Holy Spirit's release to work in your life...

to minister to others with powerful effectiveness.

This call to "more," is the call to **surrender**:

Surrender of everything.

No more holding back.

No more holding on.

No more calling the shots.

Letting go of everything...to Him.

This is an invitation to surrender your entire life: hopes, dreams, relationships, family, finances; the good, the bad, the ugly; your vocation, location, your future, your past, your present, your goals, your appearance, your health, your ministry...and if you can think of more items, then, the surrender of those as well.

- Read about the amazing event that took place in Luke 5:1-11. What two things did Jesus tell the men in verse 10?

  ▪ _____

  ▪ _____

- From verse 11 in the passage above, how did Peter, James, and John immediately respond to Jesus?

  _____

Why is it that we find it so astounding that these men forsook everything to make following Jesus their life's pursuit? And, why is it that we tend to put the "cart before the horse," so to speak. We want the Lord to give us our heart's desires without really making Him our desire and our delight?

Why are we so fearful that complete abandonment and surrender to Him might mean a life of doing what we don't want to do? It all goes back to the Garden of Eden where two things haven't changed from that time until now:

- Our finite human nature will always want to "play" God and make our own decisions that we think are best, and...
- Our adversary, the devil, speaks the same *lie* to us that he told Adam and Eve: "God is holding out on you."

There comes a point in every Christian's life (actually, every day of our lives) where a decision will be made. Are we following Jesus for what He can do for us, or are we following Him for *who He is*? Like Peter and his friends, are we willing to forsake all to follow Him?

- Please ponder the above paragraph and record what it speaks to your heart:

  _____
  _____
  _____
  _____

- Read 2 Corinthians 8:9. What do you think Paul is saying about Christ becoming *poor* that we might become *rich*?

  _____
  _____
  _____

How could we possibly think that we really know what is best for our lives, or think that He is holding out on us? Our all-creative, boundless-loving God, who made us, "wired" us, and put us together knows the beginning from the end of *everything*. He willingly left heaven's glory, suffered and died for us. Why do we think that He would not have the most exciting, satisfying, and fulfilling Life Journey possible for us? (Notice, I didn't say *easy* life...but who wants tame or dull?)

And yet, what if He *didn't* have that marvelous life for us? Would He be enough for us to abandon our lives to?

* Turn to Matthew 10:37-39. What do you think Jesus means when He states, *"...he who loses his life for my sake will find it?"*

_____

_____

_____

_____

_____

These words of Jesus are very strong words, but they are the heart of the Christian walk. They are a call to us to lay down at His feet our hopes, dreams, relationships, material goods...everything.

Yes, to genuinely follow Jesus is costly. He is not saying in these verses not to love the people in our beautiful, God-given family relationships; but He is saying that *nothing* can be more important in our lives than *Him*. Peter still loved his family *Matthew 8:14*, but Jesus came first.

The irony is that when we do lay down every aspect of our lives to Christ, *especially* family and relationships, He is then free to work His miraculous power, love, and healing into every seam of our existence. We exchange our broken lives and fractured dreams for His life: a life that is so abundant, overflowing, saturated with joy and provision, that even when our journey takes us through dark and treacherous valleys, He is more than enough for any need we might have *Psalm 23:4-6; Jeremiah 17:7-8.*

* Read Matthew 6:25-33. What does verse 33 speak to your heart?

_____

_____

_____

_____

- What do you think Jesus means when He uses the word *all* in the passage above?

Our Lord Jesus exemplified perfect surrender on the night of His betrayal:

> *"He went a little farther and fell on His face, and prayed, saying, "O My Father, if it is possible, let this cup pass from Me; nevertheless, not as I will, but as You will.""*
> Matthew 26:39

> *"Again, a second time, He went away and prayed, saying, "O My Father, if this cup cannot pass away from Me unless I drink it, Your will be done.""*
> Matthew 26: 42

Possibly it is these very words that cause us to be afraid to surrender *all* to Him. We wonder what Jesus might ask of us! Rather, these words were meant to encourage us. We won't *ever* have to endure what Jesus did; He is the only Savior. However, because Jesus suffered the beyond-words-horror of bearing our sin on the cross, we can be certain that He has already gone before us and will give us the power, strength, grace, ability and yes, absolute joy to do whatever He might ask of us *Hebrews 4:14-16, John 1:6*.

> *"Then He said to them all, "If anyone desires to come after Me, let him deny himself, and take up his cross daily, and follow Me.*
> *For whoever desires to save his life will lose it, but whoever loses his life for My sake will save it.*
> *For what profit is it to a man if he gains the whole world, and is himself destroyed or lost?"* Luke 9:23-25

- LOL! What do you think the word *daily* means in the verses above? _____

The Lord wants all of us, all of the time: 24-7-365!! Think about it. Have our "track records" been that great in comparison to His? What in the world are we waiting for? This part of the Journey, and the Journey hereafter, is based on the "ruthless trust" that the Lord Jesus is capable of caring for everything that encompasses our lives as we follow Him completely. He wants nothing less than *all* of us.

The apostle Paul knew firsthand what it was like to surrender his life to Jesus. He lived life full-throttle for Christ and his stories and letters in the New Testament are the ones that we marvel at and admire. He was at the top of the *ladder of success* when it came to Hebrew culture, but he laid down everything concerning his life to follow Jesus. He was eventually martyred for his faith. Read his words below:

> *"Yet indeed I also count all things loss for the excellence of the knowledge of Christ Jesus my Lord, for whom I have suffered the loss of all things, and count them as rubbish, that I may gain Christ..."*
> Philippians 3:8

- From these verses above, what was the most important thing in Paul's life?

  _____

  _____

- Use some of your own descriptive words that would describe what Paul called the *rubbish* of his life without Christ.

  _____

  _____

  _____

Truthfully, most of us would have no problem dying for our Lord Jesus; our problem lies in *not truly living* for Him!

* Honestly, are you at place to make the same statements that Paul did regarding the important *things* and *goals* of your life? Explain, whatever your answer might be (you don't have to share with your partners if you are not comfortable doing so!):

_____

_____

_____

_____

There is no condemnation here. We are all at different phases of our Journey. Jesus continually calls us to abandon our lives to Him, even when we don't want to. The problem is, we are the ones who lose out, miss out, and delay the blessing that fully surrendering to Christ brings.

Jesus' salvation is free. His love is free. His forgiveness is free. His grace and mercy are free. But, to truly know Him; to gain Him; is not cheap...it *will* cost us everything. But is there any other way that we would want to live?

Now for another "zinger." He wants more....

Besides desiring for us to surrender every aspect of our lives to Him, Jesus wants to be Numero Uno when it comes to our *affections* as well. Back to the beginning of this chapter, He wants to be our *delight*. He wants our hearts.

* Read John 15:9-17. From verse 9, what is Jesus inviting you to do?

_____

* From the same passage, what are the three promises given in

verses 11 and 16, when we make the Lord the *love* of our lives?

- _____
  _____

- _____
  _____

- _____
  _____

We have read before that Jesus said that the greatest thing we can do, is to love Him with all of our heart, soul, mind, and strength *Mark 12:30*. He desires a love relationship with us, not a business relationship. He wants all of our heart and affection.

If you are not sure that you have yet surrendered to the Lord Jesus in this manner, ask Him to help you. This is the Holy Spirit's delight: to reveal Jesus to us *John 16:14-15*. When the Spirit does this (and He will if we ask Him), surrendering our lives to Jesus' love is the only choice that makes sense for us.

If it sounds like you are jumping off of a cliff, well, you are! Surrendering everything to Him, means making yourself completely vulnerable to His working. That is why lifting our hands in worship is so powerful. As the universal sign of *surrender*, we are telling the Lord that He can have all of us. We are not trying to protect ourselves – He alone is our Lord and defender.

In closing, look to the beginning of this chapter at the Hebrew word *Anag* that is the definition for ***delight***. What a curious thing: part of its definition is *to be soft, to be delicate*.

When all is said and done, to walk closely with Jesus, pursuing Him and His desires alone; laying aside our will for His, is to ***walk softly****** with Him. What He says, goes. No questions asked. To take exquisite delight in Who He is, and to rejoice in His limitless love. He alone is worthy of our full surrender.

As shared by missionary Jean Firth, 1981.

 # Notes

In Over Your Head

~The Beauty of Baptism~

Together Time:

- Spend some time inviting the Lord into your time together.

- Share with one another if you have recently surrendered to the Lord something very important to you.

- Has the Lord walked you through a difficult part of your Journey lately? If comfortable, please share with one another so that everyone may be encouraged.

- Share from the lesson below, using the Notes section or margins to record meaningful words that your partner(s) might say.

Lesson:

Going under...washing off the grime, the filth, the stuff that has held you down. Dying to the old, the heavy weights, the chains that have bound you.

Rising up! Identifying with your new life in Jesus, refreshed and sparkling. No looking back, surrendered; at peace and energized all at the same time.

These are some descriptions of the power of water baptism.

What does *baptism* mean in the original language of the New Testament?

Baptizo Greek – Meaning: to baptize, to dip, dye, immerse, plunge, submerge, inundate, flood, swamp, soak, douse, drench, saturate. The semantic pliancy of *baptizo* allows it to be used in at least three distinct ways:
Materially: To immerse, dip, inundate, flood, swamp, soak, douse, drench, saturate;
Ceremonially: To wash cleanse, bathe, perform an ablution;
Figuratively: To imbue, overwhelm, sate, satiate, envelop, engulf.*

To set the stage, we see first that water baptism is an important command from the Lord.

> *"And Jesus came and spoke to them, saying,*
> *"All authority has been given to Me in heaven and on earth.*
> *Go therefore and make disciples of all the nations, baptizing them in the name of the Father and of the Son and of the Holy Spirit,*
> *teaching them to observe all things that I have commanded you; and lo, I am with you always, even to the end of the age." Amen."*
> Matthew 28:18-20

- In your own words, what does Jesus tell us to do from these verses? _____
_____
_____
_____

In the Old Testament we understand that ceremonial cleansing by water was an important element in the ministry of the priests in the temple. We all realize the importance of good personal hygiene! Whew! It doesn't take long on a crowded bus to figure out who missed the 'ole shower! Such cleanliness is important to God, too. Possibly not for the reasons we may think, but for the symbolism of being clean in our hearts and souls before Him.

• Read Exodus 30:17-21. What does this passage state regarding the Lord's priests before they could come to the altar?

_____

_____

The bronze laver filled with water for cleansing was a crucial piece of furniture in the Old Testament temple where God met the priests. These priests would not think of entering into God's presence without first washing thoroughly.

We do not see water baptism in the Bible until the appearance of John the Baptist who was Jesus' birth cousin *Luke 1:13*. All four gospels record John's ministry as a prophet in the spirit and power of the mighty Old Testament prophet, Elijah.

Many of the Old Testament prophets were led by God to do physical acts that portrayed spiritual truths. Such as, Jeremiah being told to go to the potter's house *Jeremiah 18:1-6,* signifying God's sovereignty; and Hosea being led to marry a prostitute *Hosea 1:2* to reveal God's love for His wandering people. John is led by God *John 1:33* to initiate water baptism, in bringing people into cleansing repentance in preparation for the coming Messiah: Jesus.

• Read Luke 1:5-25. List the various attributes that the angel speaks to Zacharias about his son, John. in verses 15-17:

  ▪ _____

  ▪ _____

- _____
- _____
- _____
- _____
- _____
- _____

John does indeed pave the way for the coming Savior, and he is not subtle about it! Talk about a "bull in a china shop!"

- Read Matthew 3:1-17. Record what you think you might have experienced if you had been on the banks of the Jordan listening to John preach:

_____
_____
_____

- If you had lived in New Testament times, how would you have felt if your daughter had brought John home for dinner!

_____
_____

Okay, that question was for fun...now answer these questions from the same passage:

- From verses 5-10 consider carefully why the symbolism of baptism was important. Write down your thoughts:

_____
_____
_____

- From verse 16 and 17, list the three significant things happened when Jesus came up from the water.
  - _____
  - _____

53

■ _____

• From the passage you just read, what speaks personally to your heart?

_____

_____

_____

_____

> *"John answered, saying to all, "I indeed baptize you with water; but One mightier than I is coming, whose sandal strap I am not worthy to loose. He will baptize you with the Holy Spirit and fire."*
> Luke 3:16

The Lord Jesus would indeed come to baptize His church in the Holy Spirit and fire! However, at the outset of His miraculous earthly ministry, He first took it upon Himself to be baptized by John.

Jesus, sinless and faultless, gave us the example of obedience to God; He was fulfilling all righteousness, though He Himself was righteous. Water baptism for Him represented His coming death and burial; then His rising from the curse of death. The coming of the Holy Spirit in the form of a dove announced the power of Jesus' miraculous ministry and that He would be the administrator of the baptism in the Holy Spirit upon those who would come to saving faith.

Our opening scripture for this chapter, found in Matthew, includes the "Great Commission" of Christ. This commission entails the preaching of the gospel of His shed blood for the cleansing of sin for all who would believe.

The recording of this same commission, found in Mark 16:15-16, also includes the command that Jesus' followers be baptized. However, it is clearly evident that water baptism is not essential for a person's salvation. Baptism is *very* important, but it is not a pre-requisite for the forgiveness of our sins. Jesus' shed blood alone atones for our sins *Ephesians 1:7*. We cannot "work" or earn our salvation (do an action, such as baptism); it is the gift of God's grace alone, that saves us *Ephesians 2:8-9*.

But why is water baptism so important?

- Read Romans 6:1-7. Does this give you a glimpse into the meaning of baptism? Explain.

_____

_____

_____

_____

> *"In Him you were also circumcised with the circumcision made without hands, by putting off the body of the sins of the flesh, by the circumcision of Christ,*
> *buried with Him in baptism, in which you also were raised with Him through faith in the working of God, who raised Him from the dead.*
> *And you, being dead in your trespasses and the uncircumcision of your flesh, He has made alive together with Him, having forgiven you all trespasses,"*
> Colossians 2:11-13

- Drawing from the Romans 6 passage above and the verses you just read, what does it mean for you to be *buried with Him* and *raised with Him*?

_____

_____

_____

_____

_____

Baptism is the outward sign of the inward truth that we have experienced. Water baptism is our statement to ourselves, to others, to God, to the world, and to the devil, that we believe Christ's death is enough to pay for our sin.

Our immersion into the water signifies the finished work of the Lord Jesus on the cross, identifying our sin as having died with Him. When we rise from the water, we are indicating our belief that His resurrection gives us the power to live in the newness of His life, free from sin. In many parts of the world, the act of baptism is cause for a death warrant because it is the active demonstration of faith in Christ Jesus.

- Read Acts 8:26-39. What does Philip say is the prerequisite for baptism in verse 37?

  _____

  _____

How beautiful is the simplicity of the gospel! The Ethiopian eunuch clearly understood what water baptism signified.

This raises a question for us regarding infant baptism. A study of the scriptures reveals that whenever water baptism is spoken of, it is in regard to those who have an understanding of the gospel of Jesus Christ and have received this truth into their hearts. Baptizing infants or those of an age too young to understand what they are doing is never mentioned.

God looks upon our hearts and the intent of a parent to raise their child with the knowledge of Him would not go unnoticed by the Lord.

This type of "dedication" of an infant to God is surely a blessing to His heart. Still, water baptism was meant as an outward testimony of a person's inward decision to follow Christ.

If you were baptized as an infant, praise God for parents who were dedicating you to Him. However, now that you understand the significance of this important act, please consider being baptized again as a point of obedience to the Lord and a testimony of your faith to all who see.

This is one time on your Journey of Life in Jesus when being in over your head is a good thing! Indeed, an excellent thing! Just as Jesus experienced three significant events upon His water baptism, we too can anticipate: heaven being opened to us in greater awareness of God's presence; a greater measure of the Holy Spirit in our lives; and the affirmation that we are God's child and that He is very pleased with us. Consider joining in this act of obedience as soon as possible, you won't regret it!

As Paul states…

> "I have been crucified with Christ; it is no longer I who live, but Christ lives in me; and the life which I now live in the flesh I live by faith in the Son of God, who loved me and gave Himself for me."
> Galatians 2:20

As songwriter Amy Grant has written:

> Quick sand, my heart is sinkin`
> I try to run
> But I can`t stop thinkin`
> I`m climbin` walls, I`m on the ceilin`
> It`s gonna take a miracle to heal me

I`m starin` down, into the quarry
I see a stone, for every sorry
I`m on the edge
I`m goin` under
And after I die
I`m`gonna rise from the water

I wanna blast off, let gravity disappear
I`m tired of fallin`, fallin`, fallin` from the weight of fear
Come and lift me up into the clean and clear
I`m waitin` on you, Jesus, in the water here
So come and wash me clean

The sky is red, there`s blood on my hands
I can`t deny, I`m guilty where I stand
The verdict`s in, ,I hear them shoutin`
Send me a river to drown this mountain

I wanna blast off, let gravity disappear
I`m tired of fallin`, fallin`, fallin` from the weight of fear
Come and lift me up into the clean and clear
I`m waitin` on you, Jesus, in the water here
So come and wash me clean...

Amy Grant: *Greatest Hits 1986-2004*, The Water, A & M Records, 2004.

* Spiros Zodhiates, Th.D, Editor; *Hebrew-Greek Key Word Study Bible* (Chattanooga, TN: AMG Publishers, 1996), page 1597 Greek-*Baptizo #966 NT.*

 # Notes

Shout it From the Mountaintops

~Sharing Your Faith~

Together Time:

- Open your time together thanking God for good things He has recently done for you.

- Tell about a time when you shared your faith with someone and they responded positively (in other words, they didn't unfriend you in Facebook!).

- Share about those who planted "seeds" in your life that helped bring you into a walk with Jesus.

- Share your notes from the study in this chapter. Be sure to write down or underline, meaningful phrases that are shared.

Lesson:

This lesson has the potential of going in two diverse paths.

One path can bring a sigh of relief and hope, and the other path might hold a "bummer" feeling of guilt.

The Lord wants you to experience the first path of this mountaintop adventure. Decide in your heart right now that this is the path you are choosing, and the other "bummer" path can, well, go where it leads...to you know where!

This lesson is about the exhilaration of sharing your faith with others. You may not shout it from the mountaintops so-to-speak, but you are guaranteed a mountaintop experience when the Holy Spirit uses you as a "stepping stone" or "seed planter" for someone to come to Christ.

We read in the previous chapter about the thrill of being immersed in water to declare outwardly what has taken place for us inwardly. We also started that chapter with what has been dubbed *The Great Commission* which is the proclamation of the gospel of Jesus Christ to the world. Let's read another version of this commission found in Luke:

> *"Then He said to them, "Thus it is written,*
> *and thus it was necessary for the Christ to suffer*
> *and to rise from the dead the third day,*
> *   and that repentance and remission of sins*
> *should be preached in His name to all nations,*
> *beginning at Jerusalem.*
> *   And you are witnesses of these things."*
> Luke 24:46-48

- The last sentence in the passage above is the key to sharing with others. What does it mean to be a "witness" (think crime scene)?

_____

_____

_____

_____

_____

_____

There you have it! We could end the chapter right now and you would have all that you need to know about sharing your faith in Christ. All that the Lord is commissioning us to do is to share what we know and what we have experienced about the extreme love of God and His provision through His Son's shed blood to bring us back to Him. We don't have to have a ton of Bible verses memorized and all the right words, we only need to share what we have experienced for ourselves. That is it! And, that is enough!

Why is that enough? Because no one can take away from you what you have personally experienced. No one can say to you that your experience didn't happen. Because you are a *witness* to God's touch on your life, you can speak with confidence that it is the truth.

Yes, you will gain more and more confidence in sharing your faith when the power and authority of the Scriptures continually increases in your life, but most of all, "witnessing" means naturally sharing – not forced – your personal experience with the living Lord Jesus.

Believe it or not, Paul felt that he was not a very good spokesman.

- Turn to 1 Corinthians 2:1-5. List all of the ways Paul describes his speech:

  _____

  _____

  _____

- From the same passage, why does Paul say it was **good** that his speech wasn't the best?

  _____

  _____

- **Who** does Paul say was powerful and convincing, verses 4?

  _____

- Why does Paul say the Holy Spirit was convincing?

  _____

  _____

Paul was convinced that his oratory skills weren't all that great, however, he did have confidence in the power of the Holy Spirit. It is the Holy Spirit that does all of the work when it comes to sharing our faith with others. We get all tied-up-in-knots when we think we have to do the "job." But, it is the Spirit's assignment to give testimony of Jesus; we only have to cooperate with Him *John 16:14-15*. Let's read the verse immediately following *The Great Commission* passage that we read at the start of this chapter; starting where we left off:

> *"And you are witnesses of these things.*
> *Behold, I send the Promise of My Father upon*
> *you; but tarry in the city of Jerusalem until you*
> *are endued with power from on high."*
> Luke 24:48-49

- From the verse above, Who do you think is the Promise of the Father? _____

As we learned in Chapter 5 of CrossPointe #1, every Christian has been absolutely filled to the "brim" of their spirits with the Holy Spirit. But as we also learned and just now read, Jesus told His disciples – who were also filled with the Spirit *John 20:22* – to wait for the baptism or overflow of the Holy Spirit before they proceeded to preach the gospel to the ends of the earth. Now that we have learned what water *baptism* means from the previous chapter, we can apply the same definition to the *baptism* in the Holy Spirit! The same Greek word for *baptism* is used:

Baptizo Greek-Meaning: to baptize, to dip, dye, immerse, plunge, submerge, inundate, flood, swamp, soak, douse, drench, saturate.

Jesus knew that we would need all the help we could get to be able to share our faith effectively with others. He sent the Helper – the Holy Spirit – to saturate our lives so that His overflow would reach those who don't yet know Him. If you are not sure you have experienced the Holy Spirit in this manner, simply ask Him to overflow your life; it is that easy and it is the Lord's desire for you! *Luke 11:9-13.* (It may also be helpful to review Chapter 5 from *Building a Firm Foundation.*)

Let's look at a few more verses in regard to the Holy Spirit's help in sharing the gospel with others.

• Turn to Matthew 10:16-20. Hopefully you won't ever find yourself in this situation! However, what is encouraging regarding sharing your testimony found in verses 19-20?

_____

_____

• Read Acts 4:8-10. Peter is being questioned about his faith (much like we are sometimes!). What is said here about Peter?

_____

> *"Nevertheless I tell you the truth. It is to your advantage that I go away; for if I do not go away, the Helper will not come to you; but if I depart, I will send Him to you.*
> *And when He has come, He will convict the world of sin, and of righteousness, and of judgment;*
> *of sin, because they do not believe in Me;"*
> John 16:7-9

• Who is it that does the work of convicting or convincing people about sin and righteousness? _____

You got it! The Holy Spirit does. Whew! That "takes a load off!" All we have to do is cooperate with Him. We do not have to convince or persuade anyone. In fact, if we try to do so in our own strength, we will almost always mess things up and get in the way. All we have been asked to do is share what we personally know; any convincing or persuading is the Holy Spirit's job. The ultimate decision to follow Christ will be made by the person and we can't make it for them.

> *"But even if our gospel is veiled, it is veiled to those who are perishing,*
> *whose minds the god of this age has blinded, who do not believe, lest the light of the gospel of the glory of Christ, who is the image of God, should shine on them.*
> *For we do not preach ourselves, but Christ Jesus the Lord, and ourselves your bondservants for Jesus' sake.*
> *For it is the God who commanded light to shine out of darkness, who has shone in our hearts to give the light of the knowledge of the glory of God in the face of Jesus Christ.*
> *But we have this treasure in earthen vessels, that the excellence of the power may be of God and not of us."*
> 2 Corinthians 4:3-7

- Think of your *before Christ* days. How do you think your heart was "veiled" from knowing Jesus?

  _____

  _____

  _____

- From the passage above, who is blinding non-believers?

  _____

65

- What do think is the *treasure* Paul is talking about?

  _____

  _____

- We are the *earthen vessels* spoken of here. Give some other modern-day descriptions that could also apply to us!

  _____

  _____

  _____

It is very important to realize that Satan is the one blinding unbeliever's minds and hearts. This helps us to pray more effectively for those we are trying to reach, and for us to not get upset at them, but at him! We can take authority over the enemy in people's lives through Jesus' name *Luke 10:17-20*. Also, what a comfort and joy to know that the light of Jesus (think joy, peace, love) in our hearts is our greatest testimony. His light is a wonderful treasure in us, though we may consider ourselves ordinary peanut-butter jars and not a fancy, expensive vase!

Yes, there are Christians that God has appointed as *evangelists*; those who have a special calling and Holy Spirit anointing to lead others to Christ *Ephesians 4:11-12* Yet, *The Great Commission* was given to *all* of us. Being a witness causes pure pleasure and joy and the Lord doesn't want us to miss out. We may be the only person someone might ever listen to!

- Turn to 1 Corinthians 3:5-7. What do you think Paul is saying here?

  _____

  _____

  _____

  _____

Your sharing your faith with someone may be one of many seeds planted in a person's life before they actually take the step of committing their life to Jesus.

Let's look at some examples from the Bible of people sharing their faith:

- Read John 1:35-45. In the two situations mentioned here, who are the two men who introduced people to the Lord?

  _____

- From the same passage you just read, what did Andrew do in verse 42?

  _____

How simple is that? Both Andrew and Philip had just met Jesus! They didn't know a whole bunch of stuff. They only knew that Jesus was extraordinary and they were excited about meeting Him. They only shared what they *knew* at the time. Then, they gave an opportunity for their friends to meet Jesus personally. For you, that might mean inviting them to pray with you to receive God's gift of forgiveness and salvation. Or, it may be that you extend an invitation for them to attend a Christian event or come to a church service when it seems like the right time (the Holy Spirit will help you with timing!).

If somehow you have come to a place in your Journey with Jesus where you feel like you don't have anything to share, this might be a small "temperature gauge" that your alone and intimate time with Jesus has slipped some. Joy, love, and peace have nothing to do with circumstances, but everything to do with spending time in God's Word and in His beautiful presence. No guilt here, just truth that we all need to be reminded of!

In Acts 10 we read a wonderful story of Peter being called to share Jesus with a Roman centurion named Cornelius and his family.

- Read Acts 10:44-48. What happened to those listening to Peter's words?

  _____

  _____

  _____

- Would you say that family was "ripe" to hear the gospel preached? _____

This instance gives us encouragement that the Holy Spirit knows who is "hungry" to know Jesus Christ. If you read all of Acts 10, you will find that Peter would have thought Cornelius would be the last person who would want to hear the gospel. If we are sensitive to the soft inklings the Spirit puts in our hearts and minds, we'll start to recognize who might be ready to be encouraged by what we have to say.

> *"Now while Paul waited for them at Athens, his spirit was provoked within him when he saw that the city was given over to idols.*
>
> *Therefore he reasoned in the synagogue with the Jews and with the Gentile worshipers, and in the marketplace daily with those who happened to be there...*
>
> *And they took him and brought him to the Areopagus, saying, "May we know what this new doctrine is of which you speak?"*
> Acts 17:16-19

- From the verses above, in what two places did Paul share his faith?
  - _____
  - _____

- In your own life, where is a place that you go almost daily, like

Paul did the synagogue? _____

- Name a place where you go occasionally, such as Paul did the
marketplace? _____

Your answer may have been work or school for the first question above; and maybe the mall, Starbuck's or a market for the second question. The point is that Paul was aware of those in his circle of influence on a daily basis, and with those whom he might only have one-time or occasional encounter. By just noticing those around him, the Holy Spirit could use Paul to initiate conversations in natural surroundings.

The same is true for us. It is not a mistake that we live in the neighborhoods we live in, live in our kids' school districts, work at our workplaces, or tend to shop at the same stores. There is a reason for us being there, and it *may* be to share our faith with those who are away from Christ. Begin asking the Lord to show you if you are to gently plant seeds in the soil of someone's heart or if there are any "ripe and ready" lives in your circle of influence right now. You might be surprised. Don't "freak out" or be afraid to talk to those around you, the Holy Spirit has *promised* to help you:

> *"For God has not given us a spirit of fear,*
> *but of power and of love and of a sound mind."*
> 2 Timothy 1:7

- How does the verse above encourage you in regard to sharing your faith with someone?

_____
_____
_____

This verse from 2 Timothy is powerful for practically every situation in your life (not just sharing or witnessing!), and is worthy of being underlined in your Bible! However, for the topic we are studying, this verse encourages us that when sharing our faith, we have nothing to fear.

We don't have to force anything. If the Spirit prompts us to talk to someone, we can give our fears to Him, and He will give us the power to lovingly say the right thing. And for those times when the Holy Spirit tells us *not* to say anything, we can have confidence that He knows what He is doing and knows the current state of an individual's life and heart.

Ultimately, our biggest testimony will be our lives and how we live them. If the world doesn't see any difference in life-style between us as Christians, and those watching us, anything we say will seem hypocritical. That doesn't mean perfection, but it does mean that a difference is evident. This is huge. Asking the Lord to show us areas of our lives that don't bring Him glory is a loving response to His love and is important in our witness to those who need Him.

If you have experienced sharing your faith with someone, regardless of the results, you know that there is no thrill quite like it. It truly is a mountaintop "high" to think that the Lord used you to plant a seed of faith in someone's heart. When, eventually, you see someone commit their life to Christ, it is a gift of wonder. Jesus chose you for Himself, now He would love for you to partner with Him to see others join the Journey!

> *"You did not choose Me, but I chose you and appointed you that you should go and bear fruit, and that your fruit should remain, that whatever you ask the Father in My name He may give you."*
> John 15:16

Wooooo-Whoooooo!!!

 # Notes

Finding a
Treasure Chest

~The Power of Promises~

Together Time:

- Open your time together thanking Jesus for His promises that you have seen fulfilled in your lives.

- Share a recent promise from God's Word has given you strength for a particular situation in your life?

- If comfortable, tell each other about a promise from the Bible or about a word of promise that the Lord has spoken to you that you are still waiting for its fulfillment to take place.

- Share together your notes from the study below. Be sure to underline in your Bible any powerful promises that speak to your heart and/or situation right now.

Lesson:

Oh…My…Gosh!

You have found a treasure chest. How crazy-awesome is that? Especially if the chest is limitless and you can never get to the bottom of its contents...the treasures, gem, and jewels just keep coming and coming.

That is a fun way of looking at the subject of this chapter. However, many times, indeed, most of the time; God's unending promises to us can be the difference between joy and sorrow; being lost and knowing the way; experiencing a desert or an oasis; believing lies and knowing the Truth; suffering need and having enough; and yes, life and death.

> *"Simon Peter, a bondservant and apostle of Jesus Christ, To those who have obtained like precious faith with us by the righteousness of our God and Savior Jesus Christ:*
> *Grace and peace be multiplied to you in the knowledge of God and of Jesus our Lord,*
> *as His divine power has given to us all things that pertain to life and godliness, through the knowledge of Him who called us by glory and virtue,*
> *by which have been given to us exceedingly great and precious promises, that through these you may be partakers of the divine nature, having escaped the corruption that is in the world through lust."*
> 2 Peter 1:1-4

- From Peter's words above, how are grace and peace multiplied to us?

_____

- Let's make it personal. For you, what does it mean to *know* Jesus?

_____
_____
_____

- Two questions from the passage in 2 Peter. What **has** Jesus' divine power given us, and **how** much has been given, verse 3?

  ▪ _____

  ▪ _____

- His divine power also provides us with **exceedingly great and precious promises!** Use some of your own synonyms for the italicized words (try Thesaurus.com for fun!)

  _____

  _____

  _____

  _____

Let's look at the New Testament definitions for the words "promise" and "promised:"

Epangellomai or Epangelma Greek – Meaning: To tell, declare, to proclaim as public announcements or decrees, as to announce a message, summons, or promise. Basically meaning to announce oneself, offer one's services. To promise, to give, assurance.

Peter is telling us that God's promises are being worked out by the divine power (Greek: **Dunamis** – think dynamite!) of the Holy Spirit in our lives. As we continue to grow in knowing the Lord, believing and acting on His promises, we will be transformed more and more into His likeness!

It is estimated that there are at least 3,000 promises found in the Bible. Some estimate as many as 8,000! On our upward Journey with Jesus, we are going to need many of them to see us through and keep us moving forward. There are many books and websites that you can find online or in your local Bible store that have compiled all of these promises into topics for easy reference. These books are of great help when you might need some encouragement or know someone who does.

Let's look at some "general thoughts" about God's treasure chest of promises. Turn to the passages below and write down what speaks to your heart:

- 1 Kings 8:56:

  _____

  _____

- Joshua 21:43-45:

  _____

  _____

- 2 Corinthians 1:18-20:

  _____

  _____

- Romans 4:20-21:

  _____

  _____

There are many of God's Old Testament promises that we may take hold of for ourselves. Paul tells us in Galatians that we, too, are the "seed" of Abraham, and inherit all of the nation Israel's blessings and promises, because of our faith in Jesus:

> *"Therefore He who supplies the Spirit to you and works miracles among you, does He do it by the works of the law, or by the hearing of faith –*
> *just as Abraham "believed God, and it was accounted to him for righteousness."*
> *Therefore know that only those who are of faith are sons of Abraham.*
> *And the Scripture, foreseeing that God would*

justify the Gentiles by faith, preached the gospel to Abraham beforehand, saying, "In you all the nations shall be blessed."
So then those who are of faith are blessed with believing Abraham."
Galatians 3:5-8.

- From the passage above, what qualifies us to be recipients of Abraham's blessings?

_____

You can safely insert your name in the Old Testament wherever you see such words and names as: Israel, Zion, Jacob, Abraham, Judah, Joshua, David and any other descriptors for the nation of Israel or its kings and people. Paul also tells us in Romans 11:17 that we Gentiles (anyone who is not Jewish) have been grafted in as branches in the "tree" of God's family, and again, receive His promises and blessings as His family.

- For an example, read Isaiah 41:8-13, inserting your name as suggested above. What is your favorite *treasure* from the promises given here?

_____
_____
_____

Because Old Testament promises are for us as well, you can see the importance of reading this portion of the Bible and discovering its gems for yourself during a time of need.

Our Heavenly Father is a good, just, and gracious Father. There is no one that comes close to touching His perfection. There is no one above Him or beside Him; He stands alone in beauty, magnificence, and power. He truly is our amazing Father and loves us beyond all reason and because He is the best Abba-Daddy *Romans 8:15*, we need to note that many of His promises to us are ***conditional***.

A *conditional* promise means that we have a part to play in obeying God's words to receive a particular promise before the promise if fulfilled.

Think of it this way: You have promised your child a car of their own when they turn the legal driving age for your state. However, your child is currently only four-years-old! Conditions of being able to follow rules, learning to read traffic signs, the physical ability to reach the accelerator and breaks, possibly having good grades in school, and most of all, having the maturity level to receive your promise all have a part to play before your son or daughter is able to handle your promise.

The same is true with our perfect, heavenly Father. We, in our western culture, may not always like this fact of Scripture, but it is the truth.

Just as good earthly fathers know not to give treasures to their kids who will be careless or reckless with them, so our Heavenly Father does likewise. God is not always after our comfort and He wants us for Himself in pure love and with ever-increasing, purer character. We can always trust that He has greater purposes for us than just giving us what we want. Often, we are called to battle, to stand, to obey ruthlessly, and believe Him against all odds for these promises. He will use these times of *contending* for His promises to draw us closer to Himself.

- Let's take a look at a few of these *conditional* promises. Write what the *condition* is, and then, write the promise:

- 2 Chronicles 7:14:

_____

_____

- Psalm 81:13-14:

_____

_____

- Proverbs 3:5-6

_____

_____

- Malachi 3:10 (A tithe means ten percent of our income, yes – yikes, but what joy! More about this in a future CrossPointe):

_____

_____

- Matthew 6:6:

_____

_____

- John 15:5:

_____

_____

There will many times throughout your Journey in Jesus, where He will speak a particular word or promise to you for a given situation. He may speak directly from the Bible, or speak directly to your spirit, mind, or heart. The latter may come as simply as a *thought* that you have, but you may sense that it carries a bit more *weight* than a normal thought. It may seem like an *impression*. In other words, it will be like His voice gently pressing on your spirit, mind, or heart. It may come as a *picture* that you *see* in your mind.

Because the ways the Lord speaks to us is as individual and diverse as we are, this is very subjective to each person's walk with Jesus, and difficult to describe. Just as with a spouse or good friend, over time, we can simply hear that person sigh and we know it is them without even looking! We will continually, throughout the remainder of our lives, be learning to hear His voice speaking directly to us through His written word, or directly to us. However, God doesn't contradict Himself! Anything He would tell us will line up with what He has already said in the Bible and not contradict it!

A wonderful example of a personal promise given to someone is found in Acts 27 when Paul finds himself in the midst of a dire situation (a doomed voyage):

> *"But after long abstinence from food, then Paul stood in the midst of them and said, "Men, you should have listened to me, and not have sailed from Crete and incurred this disaster and loss.*
> *"And now I urge you to take heart, for there will be no loss of life among you, but only of the ship.*
> *"For there stood by me this night an angel of God to whom I belong and whom I serve,*
> *"saying, 'Do not be afraid, Paul; you must be brought before Caesar; and indeed God has granted you all those who sail with you.'*
> *"Therefore take heart, men, for I believe God that it will be just as it was told me.""*
> Acts 27:21-25

• From what you just read, by what means did God give Paul a promise of safety? _____

• List everything that was promised (note: Paul paid careful attention to what was said, he didn't add or take away from it!):

_____

_____

• How do Paul's final words minister to your heart about promises that God has already given to you?

_____

_____

Let's look at a few more of the 3,000 promises! Write how each promise encourages you:

- Psalm 27:1:

_____

_____

- Isaiah 26:3:

_____

_____

- Matthew 6:25-34:

_____

_____

- 1 John 5:14-15:

_____

_____

Remember this passage?

> *"And you are witnesses of these things.*
> *Behold, I send the Promise of My Father upon*
> *you; but tarry in the city of Jerusalem until you*
> *are endued with power from on high."*
> Luke 24:49

- Who is the "Promise of the Father?" _____

How amazing and beautiful that the Holy Spirit is the ultimate Promise from God! He is the one Who assures us of our salvation, that we are loved and cared for, filled with His power, and glorifies God in us!

Faith will always be the key to receiving God's treasured promises. Our faith delights His heart and is the evidence that we truly do trust Him *Hebrews 11:6*.

It is also true, that our faith in His promises will be tested. Shoot! But that is all part of the Journey. Faith in His promises, especially when people or circumstances seem to be saying something else, will always be the bridge we must walk over from one mountainside to another. As in the natural realm, when we are crossing bridges of dizzying heights, it is better to keep our eyes up, on Him, than to look at the depths of the circumstances below.

- Do you have a past promise from God, which you have forgotten to keep "looking up" for? Explain.

_____

_____

_____

_____

_____

The author of Hebrews speaks these encouraging words about our salvation, but they are also words of encouragement for every promise from the Lord:

> *"Let us hold fast the confession of our hope without wavering, for He who promised is faithful."*
> Hebrews 10:23

> *"Therefore do not cast away your confidence, which has great reward.*
> *"For you have need of endurance, so that*

after you have done the will of God, you may
receive the promise."
Hebrew 10:35-36

Oh...My...Gosh! What a wonderful Lord we love and serve. Are you ready to partake of His exceedingly great and precious promises? May it be said of each us, just as Elizabeth said to Mary:

> *"Blessed is she who believed, for there will*
> *be a fulfillment of those things which were told*
> *her from the Lord."*
> Luke 1:45

 # Notes

_____
_____
_____
_____
_____
_____
_____
_____
_____
_____
_____
_____
_____
_____
_____
_____
_____
_____
_____
_____
_____
_____
_____
_____
_____
_____
_____

Climbing to the Top

~Following His Lead in Forgiveness~

Together Time:

- Start your time together asking the Lord to really "dig deep" into your hearts about any areas of unforgiveness you may still have toward someone.

- If comfortable, share a time when you were able to forgive someone for a deep wound they inflicted upon you.

- If comfortable, share a time when someone forgave you for a hurt that you caused in their life.

- Now, share with each other from the study below.

Lesson:

Wow! What amazing things we have learned and studied in CrossPointe #2! We have traveled with the "fam," heard about the power of *car tunes*, crossed bridges, been immersed in living water, discovered delight, and found untold treasure. Now, for another essential piece of "equipment" on our Journey with the Savior to reach higher heights!

Forgiveness.

No, not His forgiveness of our sin, though that is the impetus, but our forgiving others for their wounds and hurts against us. Ouch!

We may get a little bit further down the road on our Journey without this "item," but sooner or later, the "bus" of our lives will stall, and we will wonder what happened. Our Guide, the Prince of Forgiveness, won't let our Journey continue without us dealing with the hurts in our hearts that we won't let go of. Truthfully, many Christians remain stalled their whole lives, missing the thrill of intimacy with God, because of this issue of not granting forgiveness.

"In this manner, therefore, pray:
Our Father in heaven,
Hallowed be Your name.
Your kingdom come.
Your will be done
On earth as it is in heaven.
Give us this day our daily bread.
And forgive us our debts,
As we forgive our debtors.
And do not lead us into temptation,
But deliver us from the evil one.
For Yours is the kingdom and power and the
glory forever.
Amen"

"For if you forgive men their trespasses,
your heavenly Father will also forgive you.
But if you do not forgive men their

trespasses, neither will your Father forgive your trespasses."
Matthew 6:9-15

- How important do you think our forgiving others is to Jesus, if He included it in the *Lord's Prayer*? _____

- Have you ever noticed before, the verses immediately following the *Lord's Prayer*? _____

- Why do you think forgiveness, namely our forgiving others, is such a "hot button" issue with the Lord?

  _____

  _____

  _____

Wow! We cannot *work* for our salvation, in the sense that when we forgive others we then earn our forgiveness from God, but we can certainly hinder the Lord's grace and mercy in our own lives when we don't forgive those who have wronged us.

Let's look at some definitions. First *forgive* and *forgiving*:

Aphiemi Greek – Meaning: To send forth, send away, to let go from oneself. To dismiss, to let go from one's power or possession, to let go free, to let escape. To give up; to keep no longer. Metaphorically, to release from obligation, remit; of a debt, offense, to remit the penalty of sins, to pardon or forgive debts, faults, sins, and trespasses.

Charizomai Greek – Meaning: To do a favor, show kindness unconditionally, to give freely, to grant forgiveness, to forgive freely, to pardon. To be gracious, kind, benevolent. The word is from the same root as *charis,* "grace" and the same root *chara*, "joy."

Now let's look at the definitions for *debt* and *debtor:*

Opheilema and Opheiletes Greek – Meaning: To owe. A debt which must be paid; an obligation, a service which one owes someone. A debtor. One owing money; one indebted for favors; one who is delinquent, one who fails in the performance of duty. A transgressor, a sinner, one who owes a debt.

- From the Greek definition of *forgive*, what phrase(s) speak to your heart the most?

  _____

  _____

- Do the Greek definitions of *debt* and *debtor* bring new meaning to how you perceive someone who has hurt you? Explain.

  _____

  _____

  _____

  _____

Why is it that we harbor the thought that keeping forgiveness from someone, *makes them pay?* Jesus was "spot-on" when He used the word *debtor* in His prayer. A person who has wronged us may actually "owe" us, but because they can never "pay-up" we hold them guilty by not forgiving them. Nonetheless – we make them *pay.*

Actually, we end up being the ones paying for lost joy, peace, love, and most of all, God's presence. Unforgiveness never brings good or godliness to our lives and soon our lack of forgiveness can do us more harm than the offense that was first committed.

As has been stated, this is really important stuff to Jesus' heart. On our Journey, when we refuse to forgive someone, it will be like trying to cruise a beautiful, smooth, scenic highway with a flat tire. We won't get very far, very fast. We may move forward a little bit, but our travel will always be hindered until the tire is taken care of.

- Read Mark 11:25-26. How does this strong, inescapable passage move your heart?

_____

_____

_____

One of the greatest stories of a person offering forgiveness to those who heinously wounded and hurt him, is the story of Joseph found in Genesis 37-45. Taking the time to read the impact of the full story is worthy of our attention. But the "nutshell" version follows:

Joseph was the beloved youngest son of Jacob (Israel). Jacob loved Joseph more than all of his children because Joseph was the firstborn of Jacob's favorite wife. (God has always stated that monogamy is His will, this is one reason why!).

Joseph's older brothers hated him. The brothers conspired to kill Joseph, but one of the brothers, Reuben, suggested that they throw him into a pit with no water instead, and die that way (Reuben wanted to come back and rescue him). Before the rescue could take place, when Reuben wasn't around, the other brothers opted to sell Joseph to traveling traders for money and Joseph was taken to Egypt. Mind you, Joseph knew exactly what was going on. Talk about "take your drama to your Mama!" Or, rather your Papa!

Joseph, while in Egypt, had many incredible adventures, some amazing and some horrible, but God was in the whole thing. Many years later the Lord, through Joseph, rescued *nations* from famine. Ultimately when the famine struck Jacob's family back in Canaan, Jacob sent the brothers to Egypt to get food. Jacob had thought that Joseph had died many years earlier from an animal attack (a lie from the brothers). When Joseph encountered his brothers at this time, he was overjoyed to be reunited with his family (remember, they thought to murder him?), having forgiven them completely.

- Read Joseph's response to his brothers in Genesis 45:4-8 and Genesis 50:18-21? Do you sense any residual hurt in Joseph's heart in these verses? _____

- From the same passages, how do Joseph's actions and forgiveness touch your heart?

  _____

  _____

  _____

- How do you think understanding about God's sovereignty and ability to work all things for good, helped Joseph to forgive his brothers?

  _____

  _____

  _____

Joseph's story has much to teach us and one aspect is overwhelmingly obvious: no matter what people, the world, or the devil throw at us, nothing can ever stop God from turning *anything* into His purposes *Psalm 138:8*. Only we, ourselves, can hinder God's marvelous workings in our lives. No one can *ruin* our lives, our Lord is just bigger. Turning to Him and handing over the shattered pieces of our hearts, minds, and bodies is our only, yet most magnificent hope!

- Read Romans 8:28-29. How would this famous passage aid you in forgiving those who have wronged you?

  _____

  _____

  _____

  _____

- Re-read Romans 8:29. Why would forgiving all who wrong us work toward making us more like Jesus?

_____

_____

_____

Our unforgiveness towards others will not only "stall" our Journey in Jesus, but has the potential to color every aspect of our lives.

> *"Pursue peace with all people, and holiness, without which no one will see the Lord;*
> *looking carefully lest anyone fall short of the grace of God; lest any root of bitterness springing up cause trouble, and by this many become defiled:"*
> Hebrews 12:14-15

- Turn to Matthew 18:21-35. What do you think Jesus means in verses 21 and 22?

_____

_____

_____

- From the same passage in Matthew, what do you think the story is *really* about?

_____

_____

_____

_____

- From verse 35, are words of forgiveness alone, enough? _____

- From the same verse 35, what does *from your heart* mean to you?

_____

We need to stop here, for a moment, and do some soul-searching.

- Is there anyone in your life you still struggle with forgiving? _____

We may even sense that we hold God as a *debtor* because we don't understand something that He has allowed to happen (or not happen) to us. Does it keep you from fully trusting Him? He is waiting to hear from you regarding this *Psalm 62:8.*

- Do you need to *forgive* the Lord? _____

- From what you have been reading, do you think you can start the forgiving *process,* with the Jesus' help, right now? _____

Take some time with the Lord and let Him touch your heart to forgive those who came to your mind.

Back again! We may have the grace to grant forgiveness in an instant, no problems – no questions. But the deeper, horrific hurts that have taken place in our lives (usually by family or dear friends, as they have the ability to truly wound us) may take some time. Like peeling back the layers of an onion, the Holy Spirit can peel back layers of hurt, helping us to grant forgiveness at each layer. Eventually, the forgiveness is complete, and the hurt is completely removed.

Yes, our God can do this! To settle for less, is believing that God is less! This is His heart and He has the power to help us *Isaiah 61:1, Luke 4:18.* He wouldn't have commanded us to forgive every offense and everyone, if He wasn't going to give us the ability to follow through. His example from the cross is our standard and He expects nothing less than the same from us, because He has the power to help us *Hebrews 4:14-16.* This can take place regardless if the person who hurt you has asked for forgiveness or not!

> *"And when they had come to the place called Calvary, there they crucified Him, and the criminals, one on the right hand and the other on the left.*
> *Then Jesus said, "Father, forgive them, for they do not know what they do." And they divided His garments and cast lots."*
> Luke 23:34-35

- Explain what the passage above means to you and how it causes you view *forgiveness?*

  _____

  _____

  _____

  _____

- Turn to Hebrews 4:14-16. This abundant promise applies to every area of our lives, but what does it say to your heart about Jesus' ability to help you forgive anyone for anything?

  _____

  _____

  _____

  _____

- Read Ephesians 4:26-27. Assuming that something that would cause anger, needs to be forgiven, What do you learn from this passage?

  _____

  _____

  _____

- From the Scripture you just read, why would *giving place* to anger or unforgiveness, also mean *giving place* to the devil?

_____

_____

_____

_____

The Lord wants us to take care of hurts right away. He doesn't want a root of bitterness to keep us from experiencing His presence. Our forgiving others is the absolute evidence of God's work in our lives and separates us from the rest of the world.

However, forgiving doesn't mean being foolish either. It doesn't necessarily mean that you are to be BFF's with someone who has a track record of wounding you, unless the Lord has told you specifically to do so by His Spirit's power . Jesus isn't asking us to be unwise; we can still maintain forgiveness *and* have boundaries with our *debtors*. That seeming paradox is an indicator of maturity in Him. Ask for counsel if you think you might need help in this area.

Another awesome occurrence takes place when we climb the mountain of forgiveness. As Jesus becomes more and more the love of our lives, His love saturates our hearts in such a way that people just don't have the power to hurt us as in the past. His love absorbs any arrows with the outcome of our compassion and prayer for those who would knowingly or unknowingly hurt us. That doesn't mean an offense might not hurt, but it does mean that we aren't devastated by it.

In conclusion, Paul sums up the heart of Christ perfectly:

> *"Therefore, as the elect of God, holy and beloved, put on tender mercies, kindness, humility, meekness, longsuffering;*
> *Bearing with one another, and forgiving one another, if anyone has a complaint against*

> *another; even as Christ forgave you, so you*
> *also must do.*
> *But above all these things put on love, which*
> *is the bond of perfection."*
> Colossians 3:12-14

- From verse 13 above, what is the main reason given here for encouraging us to forgive?

  _____

  _____

- From the same verses, how would *putting on the love of Christ daily* be helpful in how we react to hurtful events?

  _____

  _____

  _____

It was the forgiveness that Jesus offered to us for our inexcusable offenses to Him, that drew our hearts to Him in the first place. As His followers, we can do no less to others who have sinned against us.

Come on! We have beautiful vistas to see! We have amazing feasts to enjoy! We have an incredible family to love! We can't let any flat tires get in our way of following Jesus to higher heights!

Let's join Him on the mountaintops!

> *"For who is God, except the LORD? And who is a*
> *rock, except our God?*
> *It is God who arms me with strength, And makes*
> *my way perfect.*
> *He makes my feet like the feet of deer, And sets me*
> *on my high places."*
> Psalm 18:31-33

 # Notes

CrossPointe

Sue Boldt loves sharing with both small and large groups (at no charge!). She serves as the Pastor of Women's Ministries at CrossRoads Community Foursquare Church in Fairfield, CA, where the love of her life, her husband, Randy, is Senior Pastor. Her ministry passion is helping women (and men) come to know God and the freedom to be found in His love through a continually deepening relationship with Jesus. Her life's other primary joy is being mom and grandmother to her three wonderful children, their amazing spouses, and her three precious grandchildren.

Did you know that there is a "guy" version of this discipleship tool? Check out CrossFire, which correlates directly with CP.

Follow along with CrossPointe "snippets" by "liking" the CrossPointe/CrossFire Bible Study Page on Facebook!

Please feel free to contact Sue with any comments, questions, or speaking engagement inquiries or for info on starting a CrossPointe/CrossFire Discipleship Study at your own church, neighborhood or workplace! Simply email her at susanboldt@gmail.com or at www.crossroads4you.org.

Copies of CrossPointe/CrossFire may be purchased through Sue or through www.Amazon.com.

Made in the USA
San Bernardino, CA
18 September 2017